DATE DUE

APR 3 1985			
MAY 8 1985			
DEC 6 1985			
JAN 2 8 1986			
MAY 7 1986			
MAY 1 5 1987			
OCT 2 2 '88			
NOV 2 9 '90			
JAN 24 '91			
MAR 2 5 '91			

GAYLORD

PRINTED IN U.S.A.

The Fairy Tale Book of Ballet

Text by Rosanna Hansen
Photographs by Martha Swope

Preface by Beverly Sills

Publishers   GROSSET & DUNLAP   New York
A Filmways Company

Dedication

For my mother and father

Acknowledgments

I would like to extend my appreciation to all those who helped, either directly or indirectly, in creating this book.

To Charles France of the American Ballet Theatre and Leslie Bailey of the New York City Ballet, my sincere thanks for their meticulous guidance in selecting photographs. To Susan Cook, many thanks for her thoughtful suggestions and assistance.

Also, I would like to thank a young friend, Kirsten Hall, for looking at so many pictures and listening to so many stories. And to Vicky Wong, my gratitude for helping me understand what ballet can mean to a young dancer.

To my editor Nancy Hall, a very special thank you. Her advice and participation at every stage of this project have been invaluable.

Credits

Swan Lake

Swan Lake is the best known of all classical ballets, loved by dancers and audiences alike. The story of the enchanted swan princess is taken from an old German fairy tale. V. P. Begitchev and Vasily Geltser adapted the tale as a ballet. Marius Petipa and his assistant Lev Ivanov did the choreography. The music is by Peter Ilich Tchaikovsky.

The American Ballet Theatre production of Swan Lake shown in this book was staged by David Blair. Scenery by Oliver Smith; costumes by Freddy Wittop.

CAST
Odette-Odile: **Natalia Makarova**
Prince Siegfried: **Anthony Dowell**
Queen: **Lucia Chase**

Pages 10-11, chapter opener: Eleanor D'Antuono as Odette, Gayle Young as Siegfried.

Page 20 (bottom right): Valery and Galina Panov demonstrate a high lift.

Page 31 (top): National Ballet of Canada production, with Karen Kain as Odette and Frank Augustyn as Siegfried. (Far right): Anthony Dowell as Siegfried and Natalia Makarova as Odile.

The Sleeping Beauty

The Sleeping Beauty ballet is based on Charles Perrault's familiar fairy tale. Marius Petipa composed the dances for the ballet to music written by Peter Ilich Tchaikovsky.

The production of The Sleeping Beauty in this book is performed by the American Ballet Theatre. This production, which was the first Sleeping Beauty ever done by an American ballet company, had its premiere in 1976 at the Metropolitan Opera House in New York. The staging is by Mary Skeaping; scenery and costumes by Oliver Messel.

CAST
Princess Aurora: **Natalia Makarova**
Prince Florimund:
   Mikhail Baryshnikov
Queen: **Sallie Wilson**
King: **Gayle Young**
Carabosse: **Dennis Nahat**
Lilac Fairy: **Martine van Hamel**

Pages 32-33, chapter opener: Yoko Morishita as Princess Aurora and Fernando Bujones as Prince Florimund.

Page 45 (far right): Bujones as Florimund and Morishita as Aurora.

Page 46: Puss in Boots and the Bluebird are from the National Ballet of Canada production.

Page 49: Applying false eyelashes, Violette Verdy Adjusting hair ornament, Delia Peters.

The Nutcracker

One of the most popular ballets performed today, The Nutcracker is based on the story The Nutcracker and the Mouse King by E. T. A. Hoffmann. Peter Ilich Tchaikovsky, finest of all ballet composers, wrote the music for The Nutcracker. Marius Petipa and Lev Ivanov did the original choreography.

The New York City Ballet's production of The Nutcracker, which appears in this book, was choreographed by George Balanchine. The scenery is by Rouben Ter-Arutunian and the costumes by Karinska. The children in the production are students at the School of American Ballet.

CAST
Mary: **Katherine Siobhan Healy**
Herr Drosselmeyer: **Shaun O'Brien**
Nathaniel: **Peter Boal**
Nutcracker Prince: **Peter Boal**
Sugar Plum Fairy: **Suzanne Farrell**
Cavalier: **Peter Martins**
Chocolate: **Stephanie Saland, Robert Maiorano**
Candy Cane: **Victor Castelli**
Coffee: **Stephanie Saland**

Pages 52-53, chapter opener: Melissa Hayden as the Sugar Plum Fairy and Andre Prokovsky as the Cavalier.

Preface

Ballet has been a favorite art form for many years, but never has it been as popular as today. Perhaps one reason for the explosion of interest in ballet, as well as opera and classical music, is the recent televising of live productions. These broadcasts have brought the performing arts to many who would otherwise be unable to see them. Today, dancers such as Mikhail Baryshnikov, Natalia Makarova, and Anthony Dowell can perform at Lincoln Center in New York and spectators all over the country can watch the ballets in their homes.

This book includes three of the best-loved ballets: *Swan Lake, The Sleeping Beauty,* and *The Nutcracker.* Each of these great classics tells a fairy tale, but not all ballets tell stories. Many are just pure movement that is enjoyable to watch. Yet, whether the dancers act out parts of a story or perform abstract movements, what you see is the result of many years of disciplined study.

Through my work as a singer, and now as director of the New York City Opera, I have found the performing arts to be a source of great pleasure for both adults and children. I hope that this book adds to your understanding of ballet and brings you many hours of enjoyment.

Beverly Sills

Table of Contents

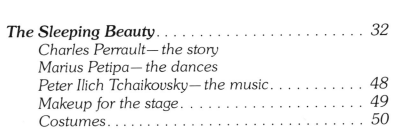

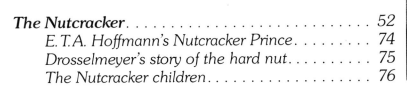

Swan Lake

$\mathcal{H}$igh in the mountains of Europe a long time ago lived a young Prince named Siegfried. On the day of the Prince's twenty-first birthday, all his friends gathered in the palace gardens to celebrate. Villagers and nobles joined together in the festivities, for the Prince chose his friends from all walks of life.

Everyone was drinking toasts, dancing, and having a wonderful time when suddenly trumpets rang out, heralding the arrival of the Queen. As she swept into the garden with her attendants, the Queen looked about with displeasure. She did not care for her son's informal ways, and disliked his choice of friends.

In a stern voice, she reminded the Prince of the seriousness of his twenty-first birthday. The following night a grand ball would be held, and there, from among the royal ladies, he must choose his bride.

The Prince grew solemn when he heard these words, but he yielded to his mother's command. Somewhat relieved, his mother presented Siegfried with her birthday gift for him—a fine new crossbow. The Prince was pleased with the handsome bow, for he loved to hunt. He thanked his mother warmly and the Queen took her leave.

Once the Queen was out of sight, everyone began to laugh and dance once more. The gay dancing no longer amused Siegfried, though, and he sat brooding about the duties that lay before him. He had hoped to marry for love some day, but now this could never happen.

His friends saw how sad the Prince had grown, and to divert him, suggested they go hunting that evening. At first they could not interest the Prince, but after much persuasion, Siegfried agreed to go.

When the hunters had walked deep into the mountain forest, they came upon a great lake shining in the moonlight. The Prince felt weary and sent the other men to search for game while he kept watch in the clearing. After they had gone, he sat alone and gazed at the night stillness of the lake.

Suddenly, from far away, a great beating of wings broke the silence. As Siegfried looked up in surprise, he saw a flock of swans flying down to the calm surface of the water. He quickly scrambled to his feet and hid where he could watch the beautiful creatures.

Delighted with his good fortune, Siegfried raised his crossbow and took aim at the leading swan. Then he hesitated, for he had never seen a creature so lovely. As the exquisite bird glided to the water's edge and stepped ashore, Siegfried nearly dropped his bow in amazement. Before his astonished eyes, the swan turned into a beautiful young woman.

With flowing grace, the swan maiden shook the water droplets from her arms and made her way toward the clearing. She wore a gown of the purest white feathers and her beautiful face was framed by a circlet of soft down. On her head gleamed the golden crown of a Swan Queen.

Siegfried was so enchanted by her strange beauty that he stepped toward her. Terrified, the swan maiden darted away from him, trying to escape.

Realizing her fear, the Prince laid down his crossbow and promised the frightened creature that he would not harm her. When she heard his oath, the swan maiden ceased trembling. She told Siegfried that her name was Odette, Queen of the Swans, but that she had once been a human princess. An evil enchanter named Von Rothbart had kidnapped her from her parents' castle. To prevent her from escaping, he had transformed her into a swan, together with her ladies-in-waiting. The enchanted swans could only return to their human form each night between midnight and dawn.

Odette explained that she would remain a swan until a man fell in love with her, married her, and promised never to love another. Only then would she be free.

Just as Odette finished telling the Prince her story, the enchanter Von Rothbart appeared and was enraged at Siegfried's presence. The enchanter transformed himself into an enormous bat and swooped down between them. But Von Rothbart was too late—Siegfried had already fallen in love with Odette. When the bat tried to attack the Swan Queen, Siegfried held her in his arms to protect her. Furious, Von Rothbart disappeared in a cloud of smoke.

With the enchanter gone, Siegfried fell to his knees before Odette and swore to her his undying devotion. The Swan Queen told him that she, too, had fallen in love.

Just then the other swan maidens came running into the clearing. The hunters, who were on their way back to join the prince, saw the swan maidens. Bows in hand, they came rushing out of the woods.

As they started to take aim, Siegfried ran toward them and ordered them to stop. Surprised at his strange behavior, the hunters reluctantly obeyed. Then, to their even greater surprise, Odette rose before them, explaining the curse of Von Rothbart. The hunters, horrified by the misfortune of the maidens, threw down their weapons.

With the swan maidens out of danger once more, Siegfried and Odette spent the remaining hours until dawn in perfect happiness.

As the first light broke through the trees, the maidens began to change from their human forms back into swans. Odette tried to linger with her beloved Prince, but the enchanter appeared once again and forced her to return.

Odette struggled bravely, but the spell was too strong. As Siegfried watched helplessly, she became a swan and soared far away into the sky.

By the time the Prince and the other hunters returned from the forest, preparations were under way for the ball that evening. All day long the ladies of the kingdom adorned themselves for the great event.

At last all was ready. What a grand affair it was to be! The great hall was lit with hundreds of candles. As people began to arrive, Prince Siegfried and his mother received the many guests. The most beautiful ladies in the world were there, each one hoping to catch the Prince's eye.

When the Queen saw how many lovely young women had come, she was greatly pleased. Surely, she thought, from such a gathering her son would find a woman who pleased him. But Siegfried's thoughts kept straying to the magic hours he had spent with Odette in the lakeside glade.

Annoyed by his inattention, his mother insisted that he dance with his guests. Siegfried tried to explain to his mother that he was unmoved by their beauty, but she became impatient with him.

In spite of the Prince's lack of interest, the festivities continued. Noble guests from other countries came forward to entertain the court with their national dances. The Spanish clacked their castanets as they danced lively flamencos; the Hungarians performed whirling czardas; the Poles, bold mazurkas.

Just as the Prince thought the dances would never end, there was a sudden fanfare of trumpets. To everyone's surprise, some late guests were announced. Into the ballroom strode a fierce-looking knight accompanied by a maiden of dazzling beauty. (Unbeknownst to the court, the strange man was none other than the enchanter Von Rothbart in a knight's disguise, and the maiden was his daughter Odile. They had conspired to make her look just like Odette.)

As the knight made his bows to the Queen, Siegfried stared at the stunning girl with great excitement. Surely, he thought with delight, this maiden was his beloved Odette. She looked just the same as when they first met, although she now wore a brilliant black gown.

So, believing that Odile was Odette, the innocent Siegfried rushed to Odile's side to dance with her. He was so bewitched by her beauty that he didn't notice her hard eyes and the way she and her father were laughing at him.

Von Rothbart smiled as he watched his daughter charm Siegfried with her splendid dancing and cunning ways. If Odile could only trick the Prince into betraying his promise to Odette, the Swan Queen would be under his power forever.

Finally the Prince, still thinking that Odile was Odette, asked her to become his bride. As he spoke, the real Odette appeared in a vision outside the window, trying desperately to warn Siegfried of the trick. However, Odile saw Odette first and stepped in front of the window so Siegfried could not see the warning.

Meanwhile, Siegfried's mother was congratulating him on his choice of a bride, and the Prince asked Odile's father for permission to marry her. The knight consented, but he told the Prince he must give a solemn oath that he would never love another woman until his death.

Siegfried was offended by the odd request and hesitated for a moment—but then he remembered Von Rothbart's curse and agreed. Instantly there was a huge crash of thunder and a great wind blew out all the candles. As the lightning flashed, Von Rothbart and Odile revealed themselves in their true forms, and laughing horribly, vanished from the room. Odette appeared once again at the window, reaching out to Siegfried helplessly and sobbing in despair.

This time, as Siegfried saw Odette, he realized in horror how he had been tricked. Now Odette and her maidens would remain swans forever. Siegfried stood in despair as the frightened guests fled the ballroom. Then, distraught with grief, he plunged into the gloomy night to search for Odette.

At the lakeside, the swan maidens anxiously awaited Odette's return, fearful for her safety. When Odette finally arrived, sobbing with grief, the maidens clustered round to comfort her. She told them that their kindness was of little use—she had been betrayed.

At that moment Siegfried rushed into the glade and threw himself at Odette's feet, begging her forgiveness. As Siegfried explained how Odile had been transformed to look like her, Odette's heart went out to him once more.

She told him she would gladly forgive him, but now she could never escape her doom—Siegfried had promised himself to another. Odette declared that she must die, for only in death would she be free of Von Rothbart's power. The Prince, knowing his life without her would be meaningless, vowed that he would die as well.

Just then Von Rothbart, disguised once more as a huge bat, loomed before the lovers to crush their act of defiance and separate them. But the strength of their love overpowered the villain.

Resolved to be together in death, the lovers embraced a final time and threw themselves into the deepest part of the lake. When the water closed over their heads, Von Rothbart fell to the ground in agony, conquered by their love.

As the dawn began to break, the swan maidens knew that the spell was broken and they would never again be transformed into swans. The spirits of Odette and Siegfried were united and would remain forever by the side of Swan Lake.

Gelsey Kirkland, shown at the far left as a student, is now a famous ballerina. (Center practice at the School of American Ballet)

BALLET CLASS

Every ballet class, for young students and stars alike, begins with exercises at the *barre*. The barre is a wooden bar or rail fastened to the walls of the studio. While they exercise, the students rest one hand lightly on the barre to help them balance.

First they do deep knee bends called *pliés,* which gently stretch and warm the leg muscles. The movements at the barre loosen the joints and prepare the muscles for more strenuous activity.

After barre work, the students move out to the middle of the room for center practice. For beginners, this is mainly a repeat of the barre exercises. As the students advance, though, they spend more time on the difficult ballet steps and positions that you see on stage.

The first part of center practice is called the *adage.* Adage, which means ''leisurely'' in French, is a series of slow movements that develop balance and control. (Since the first national school of ballet was in France, you will notice that ballet terms are always given in French.) The students work on such important poses as the *arabesque,* in which they stand on one leg with the other leg raised high in the back. To see why a dancer needs good balance, try standing in an arabesque for several minutes without wobbling.

After slow exercises, the students are ready for the last part of class—jumping and leaping. This work is called *allegro,* which means quick and lively. They start with small jumps and progress to big, dramatic leaps. This is usually the students' favorite part of class.

If the students go on to careers in ballet, they will take class almost every day of their working lives as dancers. Daily class, they learn, is essential for them to keep their muscles and skills at their best. When they become professionals, they know that if they miss class for even one day, they will notice a difference. If they miss more than one day, everyone will *see* the difference!

When they are about fourteen or fifteen years old, advanced students begin dancing together as partners. In their special classes, which are called *pas de deux* classes or "double work," the boys learn to use their strength to support and lift the girls.

To dance well together, the partners must learn to move in complete harmony. When they do a high lift, for example, they need split-second timing and coordination. The girl will breathe in just as her partner begins to lift her and will push off from the ground at the same moment. Her push makes it easier for the boy to lift her up. Once she is high above his head, he will straighten his arms and "lock" them in place to hold her securely.

A boy must develop muscles that are very strong to hold a girl's entire weight above his head. He must do exercises to build up his strength, so he can make the female seem light and easy to support.

As Peter Martins of the New York City Ballet shows with this exercise, a male dancer develops very strong muscles in his arms and legs.

Although a high lift requires great strength from the male dancer, it should look easy to do.

start to wear toe shoes
several years of lessons,
ly when they are about
n years old.

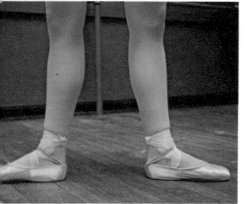

First position

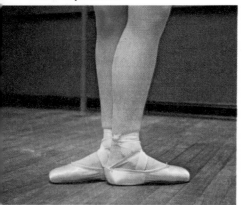

Second position

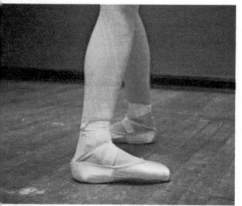

Third position

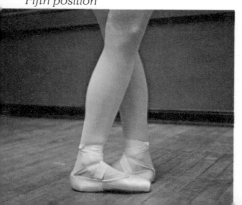

Fourth position
Fifth position

THE ENCHANTED SWAN

Swan Lake, which is based on an old German fairy tale, is the most popular of all classical ballets. When *Swan Lake* is performed, the roles of Odette and Odile are usually danced by the same ballerina. To succeed in this double role, the ballerina must be a fine actress as well as a superb dancer. As Odette, she plays the part of a sad and gentle Swan Queen; as Odile, she is an evil and powerful enchantress. Because the two characters are completely different, dancing Odette-Odile is considered a supreme test of the ballerina's art.

Odette-Odile and the swans use special arm and hand movements to suggest feathery wings. With these fluttering, quivering gestures, a dancer makes us feel that she is actually an enchanted bird.

FIVE FEET POSITIONS

All movements in ballet are based on these five positions. To do them correctly, both legs must be "turned out" from the hip. If you try placing your feet in these positions, you can feel what "turned-out" means.

←

Yoko Morishita demonstrates some of the typical swan gestures from the ballet.

PAS DE DEUX (DANCE FOR TWO)

Swan Lake is famous for the beautiful duets *(pas de deux)* danced by Prince Siegfried and Odette-Odile. When the Prince first meets Odette at the enchanted lake, they dance a slow love duet, accompanied by the swan maidens *(corps de ballet)*. In this slow pas de deux, the male dancer supports the ballerina in lovely poses, helps her turn, and lifts her high in the air to express the beauty of Odette and Siegfried's love.

Later in the ballet, evil Odile dances with the Prince at the royal ball. They perform an exciting *grand pas de deux* (literally, a grand dance for two). In this showpiece, the principal dancers display their skill with several brilliant dances. These dances always follow the same order. First there is a slow duet, followed by exciting solos for each dancer, and a spectacular finale called a *coda* that the two perform together.

In his solo, the male dancer will always perform athletic jumps and leaps that show his strength and technique. Siegfried starts his solo in the grand pas de deux by bounding out from the wings in a series of high leaps *(grand jetés)*. Without a pause, he circles the stage with a soaring chain of leaps.

These virtuoso leaps show us the dancer's technique, but they do more than just that. They also express Siegfried's tremendous excitement at finding the woman he believes to be Odette, his true love.

Odile's solo, which follows his immediately, also has brilliant steps and ends with the most famous moment in ballet history. From a single preparation, Odile performs thirty-two spectacular whipping turns *(fouettés)* on one toe—without stopping to rest. (Sometimes when you watch this solo, you can hear people in the audience softly counting up to thirty-two as the dancer spins around. Then, of course, you hear applause!) In the ballet's story, these fast, brilliant turns represent Odile's wicked pleasure at having fooled Siegfried into thinking she is Odette.

In this pas de deux and throughout the ballet, the dancers tell the story with their gestures and movements. Even though they never speak, we understand the story's meaning clearly through their actions.

Grand pas de deux

31

The Sleeping Beauty

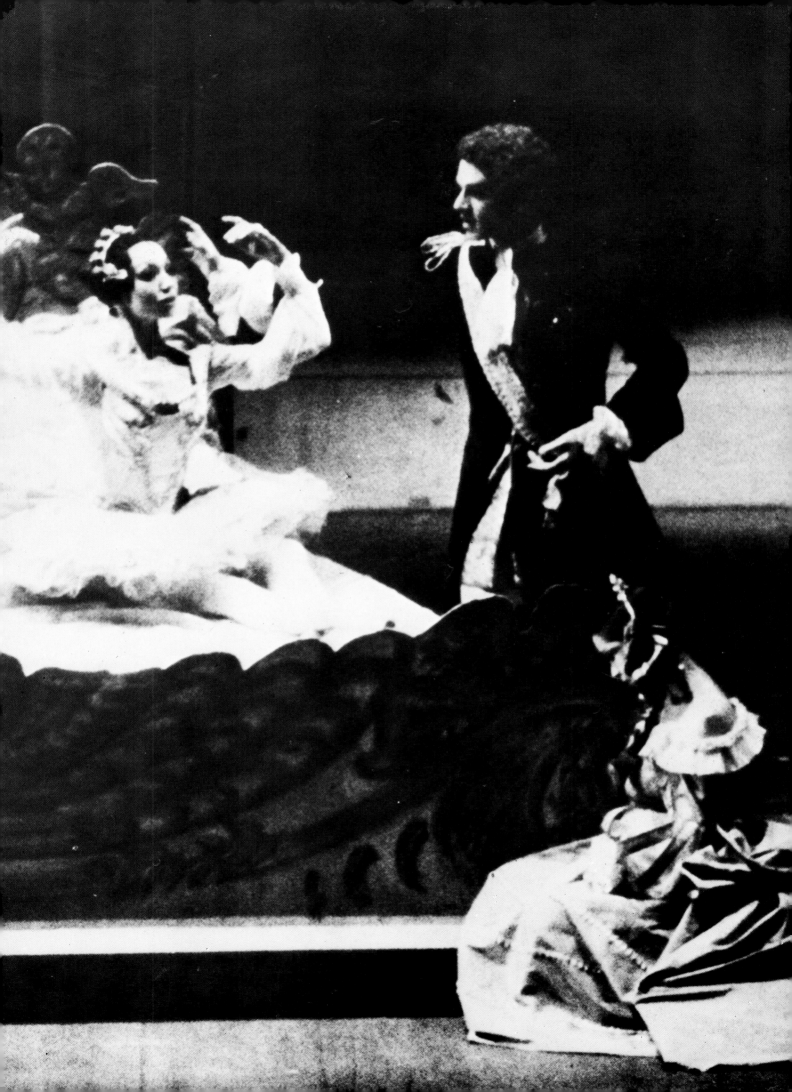

*L*ong ago in a distant land lived King Florestan and his fair Queen. The King and Queen loved each other, but because they had no children, they were sadder than words can say. For many years they made special vows, ate magic herbs, and did everything they could think of—but without success.

At last, however, the Queen gave birth to a baby daughter. They named the child Aurora after the goddess of the dawn, for her birth was truly the dawn of their happiness.

To celebrate their joy, the King and Queen announced that they would hold a grand christening party. They invited everyone in the kingdom, and asked all the fairies to be godmothers to the baby Princess. According to ancient custom, each fairy godmother would give the Princess a magic gift, blessing her with every imaginable virtue.

When the christening-day arrived, Catalabutte, the Master of Ceremonies, presented the guest list to the King and Queen, who reviewed the names and took their places on the thrones.

Even as the monarchs took their seats, trumpets heralded the first arrivals. Catalabutte greeted every guest, announcing each name to the court. Lords and ladies, dukes and duchesses, princes and ambassadors—all were welcomed with great ceremony.

When all the nobles were seated, another fanfare rang out and the arrival of the fairy godmothers was announced. After they made their bows, each fairy in turn bestowed a gift upon the sleeping Princess. The youngest fairy gave Aurora the gift of beauty; the next, wit; then grace, kindness, dance, and song.

The Lilac Fairy, who was the last to speak, floated high above the cradle to give the baby her blessing. But before she could say a single

word, a terrible roll of thunder shook the room, and a great wind tore the curtains.

As silence fell over the court, a great black coach drawn by four immense rats swept in through the window. The horrible old fairy Carabosse stepped out, looked angrily around the room, and cackled wickedly. A deadly insult had been dealt her, shrieked Carabosse. Why had she not been invited?

The King and Queen begged her forgiveness and pleaded with her to join in the festivities, but the evil fairy only laughed the more. She, too, would give the Princess a gift, said Carabosse, despite the insult to her. The Princess would indeed become the most clever, kind, and beautiful girl in the kingdom—but she would not live to be a woman. One day she would prick her finger on a spindle and die. Having spoken this curse, the wicked fairy broke into peals of horrible laughter.

Everyone shuddered when they heard these terrible words, and the Queen fainted dead away. But then the Lilac Fairy stepped forward and raised her wand against Carabosse. As the wicked old crone fell back in surprise, the Lilac Fairy said that, although she could not remove the curse, she could soften it. Aurora would someday prick her finger, but she would not die. Instead, she would fall into a deep sleep and sleep for a hundred years. At the end of that time, a prince would come to awaken her with the kiss of true love.

When Carabosse heard these words, she was so furious that she vanished in a puff of smoke. The King and Queen, who wept with joy and relief, fell on their knees to thank the Lilac Fairy. And the King, hoping to prevent the unhappy doom foretold by Carabosse, immediately issued an edict forbidding all persons, on pain of death, from using spindles or needles of any kind.

Years passed. As the fairies had promised, Aurora grew up to be clever, beautiful, and loved by all who knew her. When her sixteenth birthday arrived, the King and Queen held a great festival, and people came from far and wide to celebrate. Chief among the guests were several handsome princes who had journeyed from distant kingdoms to seek Aurora's hand in marriage.

At the appointed hour, the gates of the royal gardens were thrown open and the guests began to assemble. Villagers bedecked with flowers, nobles in their richest apparel, the foreign princes, and the King and Queen—all gathered to await the arrival of the Princess.

While the villagers danced, Catalabutte, who was once again the Master of Ceremonies, noticed three old peasant women watching the dancers. To his horror, he realized that they were knitting. He rushed over, snatched the knitting needles from their hands, and ordered them out of the palace grounds. Had they not heard the King's edict forbidding sharp objects? As the old women pleaded their ignorance, they scurried away as fast as their legs would carry them.

At that moment, Princess Aurora came running across the palace lawns, looking radiantly beautiful in her pink and silver gown. As she greeted her parents and friends, everyone was thoroughly entranced by Aurora's charm. She danced with each of the foreign princes, smiling politely as they presented her with roses. But after every dance, she handed the flowers to her mother, refusing to favor any of her suitors. She was enjoying herself far too much to bother with serious thoughts of marriage!

While the Princess was dancing, an old peasant woman wrapped in a black cloak pushed her way to the front of the crowd. When she reached Aurora's side, she thrust a golden spindle toward the Princess. Aurora was delighted with the strange object, for she had never before seen such a thing, and she danced gaily with the spindle in her hands.

Before her horrified parents could reach her, Aurora cried out in pain, for she had pricked her finger. She swayed back and forth and fell to the ground as though dead. As she fell, the old peasant threw off her tattered cloak. She was none other than wicked Carabosse, who shrieked with delight at her evil work and vanished in a cloud of smoke. While the Queen and her ladies collapsed in tears, the Lilac Fairy appeared. She reassured the King and Queen that their daughter was not dead but only sleeping. The Princess would sleep for a hundred years, said the Fairy, at which time she would be awakened by a handsome Prince.

Then, as the Fairy waved her wand over the court, everyone began to yawn, and fell at once into the deepest slumber. When everyone in the castle was asleep, the Fairy waved her wand once more. Instantly huge trees shot up, vines and creepers sprouted, and a maze of foliage twined around the castle grounds. Within an hour, a thick forest had completely hidden everything from sight. So dense and tangled was the forest that the sleeping castle lay undisturbed for many years.

A hundred years had passed when Prince Florimund was out hunting with the lords and ladies of his court. After several hours, they tired of the sport and stopped by a stream in a sunny meadow. For a new diversion, Countess Anna persuaded the Prince and lords to join the ladies in courtly dances. Soon, however, the Prince grew moody and dropped out of the dance. He felt bored with the nobles and their frivolous pleasures and had grown dissatisfied with his life at court.

When the dances ended and the hunters prepared to return to the forest, the Prince told the Countess and his other friends that he would stay behind.

The Prince had only been alone a few minutes when a golden boat came floating down the stream toward him. In the boat stood the beautiful Lilac Fairy. As the Prince stared at her in amazement, the Fairy stepped out and greeted him by name. She said that she could help him find great happiness, if he would trust her completely. The Prince eagerly agreed, and the Fairy summoned before him a magic vision of Princess Aurora.

Florimund was enchanted by the girl's exquisite beauty. He had no sooner reached out to touch her than she vanished among the wood nymphs of the forest. When he saw that the vision was gone, Florimund begged the Fairy to help him find it again. She agreed, and as she waved her wand, the Prince found himself in the middle of a dense forest. As he stepped forward, the twisted branches parted to make a path for him. Florimund followed the winding path until he reached the silent, gloomy castle.

Before him lay the motionless bodies of guards and courtiers who had fallen asleep in the very places they had stood when the spell was cast. The guards were slumped over their shields, the nobles sprawled in their chairs, and the King and Queen sat asleep on their thrones.

The Fairy appeared before him, urging him onward. The Prince pushed past the still figures and climbed the marble stairs until he came to a chamber trimmed all in gold.

There before him lay the sleeping Princess, lovely in the freshness of her youth. Spellbound, the Prince bent forward and kissed her.

At once Aurora opened her eyes, and immediately, the court awoke. The guards jumped to their feet and the King and Queen greeted the young Prince who had freed them all from the magic spell.

As the Lilac Fairy had foretold, Princess Aurora and Prince Florimund fell deeply in love and were married. Their wedding celebration was a truly splendid affair. For fourteen days and nights, there was dancing, feasting, and rejoicing throughout the kingdom.

Guests traveled from distant lands to attend the celebration, and everyone in the kingdom took part. All of Aurora's fairy godmothers were there, glittering in robes of gold, silver, diamond, and sapphire. Even Puss in Boots and the White Cat came, along with the Bluebird of Happiness and Red Riding Hood.

When King Florestan had joined the hands of Princess Aurora and Prince Florimund in marriage, the Prince and Princess delighted their guests with a joyous wedding dance. As they danced, the Lilac Fairy blessed them and granted them happiness for all of their days.

CHARLES PERRAULT—THE STORY

"Once upon a time there were a King and a Queen who were grieved, more grieved than words can tell, because they had no children." With these words, the French writer Charles Perrault began his classic fairy tale, *The Sleeping Beauty in the Wood.*

Perrault published *The Sleeping Beauty* in 1697 as part of his collection, *Stories of Times Past, or Mother Goose Tales.* He didn't seem to think very much of his new book at first and did not even publish it under his own name. Little did Perrault know that his *Stories* would become the most famous group of fairy tales in Europe. The book was an immediate success and has been loved ever since, for it contains such fairy-tale masterpieces as *Little Red Riding Hood, Bluebeard, Puss in Boots, Tom Thumb, Cinderella,* and *The Sleeping Beauty.*

Bettmann Archives

MARIUS PETIPA—THE DANCES

In 1889, one hundred and ninety-two years after Perrault wrote his tales, Marius Petipa awakened *The Sleeping Beauty* to a new life. That year, he composed the dances that would tell Perrault's famous story in ballet. When Petipa's *Sleeping Beauty* ballet was performed the next year, it was recognized at once as his most perfect work. With this beautiful ballet, Petipa showed that he was the finest choreographer (dance composer) of the nineteenth century.

Although Petipa was born in France, he spent over fifty years in Russia. During his Russian stay, he created over sixty full-length ballets and hundreds of shorter works.

Petipa used music by Peter Ilich Tchaikovsky for his three best-loved ballets: *The Sleeping Beauty, The Nutcracker,* and *Swan Lake* (which he composed with his assistant, Lev Ivanov). These magnificent ballets are a lasting monument to Petipa's genius. Although he has been dead for over seventy years, his three finest works are still performed all over the world.

PETER ILICH TCHAIKOVSKY—THE MUSIC

When Tchaikovsky was asked to compose the music for *The Sleeping Beauty,* he agreed with delight. He wrote in his letter of acceptance: "I should like to tell you straight away how charmed and enthusiastic I am. The idea appeals to me and I wish nothing better than to write the music for it." He set to work with such intensity that while he was composing the ballet, he often had dreams in which he himself was performing as a dancer.

Tchaikovsky wrote many kinds of music—operas, ballets, symphonies, and piano concertos. Of all these compositions, the ballets are his most popular works. Besides *The Sleeping Beauty,* Tchaikovsky wrote *The Nutcracker* and *Swan Lake* ballets. Today, each of these is considered a great masterpiece. Tchaikovsky, in fact, is known as the greatest composer of ballet music who ever lived.

Bettmann Archives

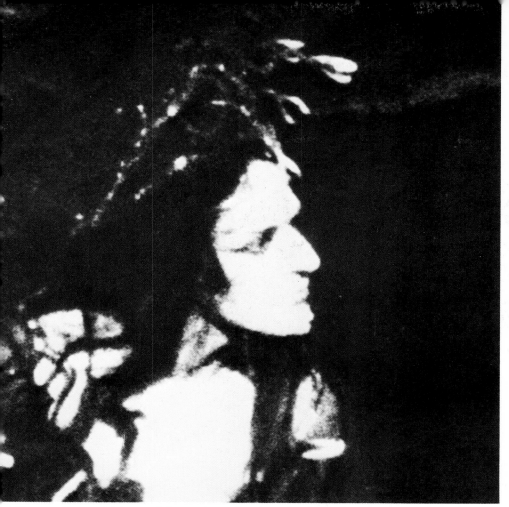

Dancer Dennis Nahat with his makeup for the role of Carabosse.

Dennis Nahat without makeup.

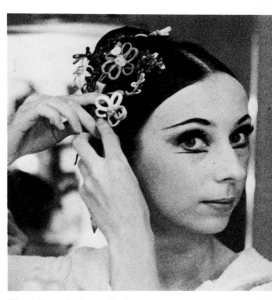

Besides doing their own makeup, the dancers also arrange their hairdos. They often wear headpieces that must be pinned securely into place.

Female dancers often use false eyelashes to accent their eyes.

MAKEUP FOR THE STAGE

Did you know that the wicked fairy Carabosse is really a man? In *The Sleeping Beauty* and other ballets, parts like evil fairies and witches are usually played by male dancers. The men use special stage makeup, wigs, and costumes to transform themselves into ugly old women.

When a dancer does his makeup for a character part like Carabosse, he first enlarges his nose and chin with "nose putty." The putty is a soft, sticky clay that can be molded to any shape, so he can make his features as big and horrible as he wants. He may also add warts and bumps of putty to other parts of his face.

When the nose putty is firmly in place, the dancer applies foundation makeup and draws lines and wrinkles around the eyes and mouth. Some shading for the lips is added, too.

Next come the eyes. He draws in huge eyebrows and exaggerates his eyes with eye liner and different shades of shadow. After a final touch of powder, the fairy looks truly evil.

A role like Carabosse calls for special, elaborate makeup, but all the dancers use basic stage makeup when they perform. Without it, the audience would not be able to see their facial features clearly.

Makeup may also be used to improve a dancer's features. For example, a dancer might use dark shading on his or her cheeks to make them look thinner. Basically, dark shading will make facial areas look smaller or shorter, and white highlights make features look bigger. With makeup tricks like these, even the less attractive dancers can make themselves look striking.

COSTUMES

Because *The Sleeping Beauty* tells the story of a royal princess, the costumes for the ballet must look rich and elaborate. To make the court costumes, the designer will use all kinds of beautiful materials: satin, velvet, silk, brocade, leather, and lots of net for the ballerinas' skirts.

Even though the court costumes look rich, the fabrics must be as light as possible so the dancers won't feel weighted down. At the same time, the cloth should be very hard-wearing to survive many performances and frequent washings.

A few of the costumes require special materials. Puss in Boots and the White Cat, for example, have costumes and masks trimmed with fur, and the Bluebird wears a headdress made of feathers. The rats who pull Carabosse's chariot have furry brown heads and long stuffed tails.

A ballet like *The Sleeping Beauty,* which requires several hundred costumes, will take months of preparation by the costume department.

The
Nutcracker

On Christmas Eve in a little town in Germany, the Mayor, Dr. Stahlbaum, arranged a special Christmas party for his daughter Mary and son Fritz. The children, dressed in their best clothes, peeked into the parlor through the keyhole and watched their parents decorating the great Christmas tree.

Soon the guests began to arrive and the other children joined Mary and Fritz to steal a glimpse of the wonderful room. Finally, the clock struck nine, and the parlor doors were thrown open. The children rushed to the tree and looked in awe at the sparkling candles and brightly colored ornaments.

After the grown-ups greeted one another, they organized games and dances for the children. While the children played, their minds wandered to the mounds of packages wrapped in shiny paper and bows.

It seemed like forever before it was time to open the presents. Mary and the other girls shrieked with delight as they unwrapped their beautiful dolls. While the boys played happily with their trumpets and drums, the girls cradled their new dolls tenderly in their arms.

Suddenly, the clock struck again and a mysterious old gentleman appeared at the door. He was Herr Drosselmeyer, a friend of Mary's family and her godfather. While most of the children were frightened by the strange old man, Mary recognized him at once and ran to greet him. Drosselmeyer hugged her and introduced her to his young nephew Nathaniel, whom Mary thought was very handsome.

Herr Drosselmeyer was quite well known as an inventor who made wonderful clockwork toys. Although the curiosity of the children was aroused by the huge boxes Drosselmeyer brought, they were too frightened to come near until he began to perform his clever magic tricks. Then, even the most timid of the children forgot his fears.

Drosselmeyer and Nathaniel opened the huge boxes and presented four life-size dolls—Columbine and Pierrot, a Turk, and a tin soldier. Drosselmeyer waved his hand, and the toys began to dance for the wide-eyed children. When the toys stopped moving, the children ran to the dolls, convinced that they were alive. But, much to their amazement, they were just dolls, after all.

Then Drosselmeyer presented Mary with a special gift just for her—a fine wooden Nutcracker made in the shape of a soldier. The Nutcracker wore a brightly painted red and blue uniform and had a big square head with a broad smile. Drosselmeyer taught the children how to crack their walnuts in the mouth of the Nutcracker.

Mary took her new Nutcracker and ran about the room, showing it to all of the children—until Fritz became very jealous and grabbed the Nutcracker from Mary's hands. As he ran away with it, Mary and Nathaniel chased after him, but naughty Fritz smashed the Nutcracker to the floor and broke its jaw.

Mary burst into tears when she saw her poor wounded Nutcracker, but Drosselmeyer comforted her. He bandaged the Nutcracker's head with his handkerchief and assured Mary that her toy would soon recover from its injuries. Then Nathaniel presented Mary with a little doll's bed on which she laid the Nutcracker to sleep.

It was growing very late, and all the children were getting tired and sleepy. After a feast of cakes and ice cream, the guests prepared to leave. When the party was over, Mary and Nathaniel said good night, but Mary secretly hoped that they would meet again very soon.

In no time at all, everyone in the household was in bed, leaving the great Christmas tree shining in the dim moonlight.

All was still, but Mary could not sleep. She tossed and turned, worrying about her wounded Nutcracker. She decided to go see if it was healed yet, and crept downstairs, being careful not to make any noise.

The parlor seemed big and strange in the dim light, but Mary bravely went straight to the Nutcracker's side. Happy to see it sleeping peacefully, she moved its bed closer to the Christmas tree and stretched out on the sofa, immediately falling asleep.

A little later, Mary awakened with a start. She heard squeaky, rustling noises, and as she rushed to her Nutcracker, the Christmas tree began to grow to enormous size. The grandfather clock solemnly struck the hour of midnight. On top of the clock, a large gilt owl flapped his enormous wings. (The owl looked just like Herr Drosselmeyer! He seemed to be waving his arms wildly as if commanding the strange events to happen.)

While Mary stared in amazement, everything in the room began to grow out of proportion. All the toys came to life and began to move about

the room. Then Mary heard a sharp whistle, just as giant gray mice ran into the room. Mary was terrified of the horrible beasts, but the Nutcracker, grown to life-size, jumped up and led the toy soldiers into battle to protect her.

The battle raged back and forth, for the mice fought fiercely. Just as the Nutcracker and his soldiers captured one of the mice, the ferocious Mouse King appeared—a frightening beast with seven heads, each wearing a golden crown. The Nutcracker and the Mouse King fought a duel, and the Nutcracker fell to the ground. To distract the Mouse King, Mary threw her slipper and hit him. But just as he whirled to attack her, she fainted and fell back onto her bed. The Nutcracker, leaping forward to save her, slew the Mouse King with his sword. Triumphant, he cut off one of the Mouse King's golden crowns and held it high in victory. As if by

magic, the Nutcracker was transformed into a handsome young Prince—
who just happened to bear a striking resemblance to Nathaniel.

At this same moment, the parlor turned into a great forest deep in
snow and ice. Controlled by unseen forces, Mary's bed whirled through
the snowy night as she slept.

When her bed came to rest in the forest, the Prince gently awakened
her and placed the shining golden crown upon her head. He thanked her
for saving his life and invited her to join him on a magical journey.

While the snowflakes danced faster and faster in the moonlight, the
Prince and Mary walked hand in hand through the forest.

Soon Mary noticed that they were no longer walking, but were flying swiftly through the air. The Prince explained that they were on their way to the Kingdom of Sweets, a magic land ruled by the Sugar Plum Fairy. A flock of guardian angels greeted them at the gates of the kingdom. Inside, Mary saw castles made of cake and cookies, high towers of gingerbread with ice cream domes, and roads of marble candy. Everything was topped with spun-sugar frosting, and Mary was sure that she had never seen such a delightful place before.

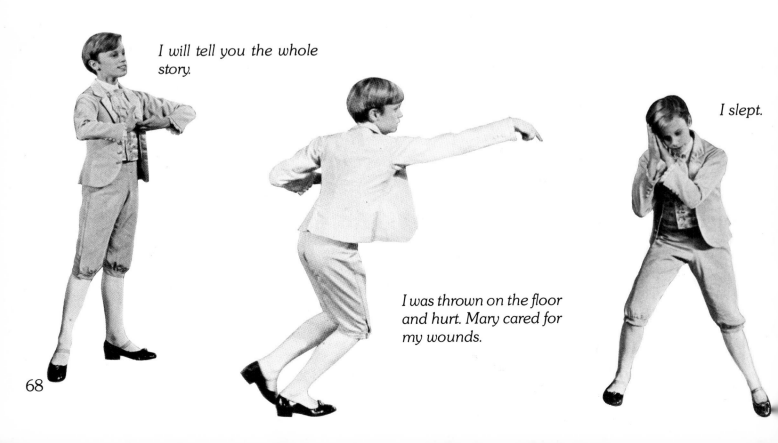

I will tell you the whole story.

I was thrown on the floor and hurt. Mary cared for my wounds.

I slept.

As she and the Prince sailed together in a walnut shell down cool rivers of lemonade, they reached the palace of the Sugar Plum Fairy.

The Prince introduced Mary to the beautiful Fairy, who asked them to tell her about their adventures. The Prince proudly told her how Mary had saved his life.

Suddenly we were attacked by huge mice. I commanded my soldiers to fight them.

The Mouse King and I fought a duel. I was losing, but Mary threw her slipper to distract the monster. He turned, and I killed him with my sword. Mary's courage saved me.

I have told you everything.

The Sugar Plum Fairy was delighted with their bravery and congratulated Mary and the Prince. She announced to the court that a celebration must be held in their honor.

As the festival began, Mary and the Prince were seated on a golden throne, before which a great table was heaped with ice creams and chocolates. Then the Sugar Plum Fairy clapped her hands, calling forth sweets and spices from distant lands to dance for her guests—there were dark chocolates from Spain, aromatic teas from China, red-and-white striped candy canes, delicious exotic coffee from Arabia, sweet shepherdesses made of marzipan, and little bonbon candies who scurried out from under the skirts of Mother Ginger. It was all so beautiful that Mary could hardly believe her eyes.

The grandest part of the festival was yet to come—the dance of the Sugar Plum Fairy and her Cavalier. Together they performed a beautiful love duet, and Mary and the Prince admired the splendor of the couple's happiness.

At the end of the celebration, the Sugar Plum Fairy and her Cavalier bade farewell to Mary and the Prince. As all the sweets and spices waved goodbye, the young couple stepped into a shining sleigh drawn by magic reindeer, and soared away into the Christmas night.

E. T. A. HOFFMANN'S NUTCRACKER PRINCE

The magical story of the Nutcracker Prince was created by E. T. A. Hoffmann, a German writer who was famous for his fairy tales. Hoffmann wrote his story, which he called *The Nutcracker and the Mouse King,* for a Christmas collection of fairy tales published in 1816.

Some of the Nutcracker story was based on Hoffmann's own life. Mary and Fritz were actually the children of one of his friends, and the mysterious Herr Drosselmeyer of the story is none other than Hoffmann himself.

Although Hoffmann wrote only sixty tales in his short life, they were known and loved by children throughout all of Europe. His stories inspired other ballets *(Coppelia)* and operas *(Tales of Hoffmann)* and influenced many authors. Today Hoffmann is considered one of the greatest fairy-tale writers who ever lived.

In 1892, Ivan Vsevolojsky chose Hoffmann's Nutcracker story for his new Christmas ballet in St. Petersburg, Russia. Vsevolojsky was the director of the Imperial Theaters in St. Petersburg, where he staged some of the finest ballets ever created. For his Christmas ballet two years earlier, Vsevolojsky had used the fairy tale *The Sleeping Beauty*, which had been an enormous success. Vsevolojsky hoped that another fairy-tale ballet would be equally popular. He asked Peter Tchaikovsky and Marius Petipa, the same team who created *The Sleeping Beauty,* to work together on *The Nutcracker*.

Petipa, the principal choreographer for the Imperial Ballet, adapted Hoffmann's tale. He found that the original story was too long for him to present it all in ballet form, so Petipa left out one whole section of Hoffmann's story.

In the part of the story that Petipa omitted, Drosselmeyer comes to visit Mary the morning after the Christmas party. He explains to her why the Nutcracker Prince and the Mouse King had become enemies, and how the Nutcracker Prince was transformed into a wooden Nutcracker. Drosselmeyer's tale, which is called "The Story of the Hard Nut," begins with the enchantment of a Princess named Pirlipat. Here is the story he told to Mary.

DROSSELMEYER'S STORY OF THE HARD NUT

Bettmann Archives

A long time ago in a little country near Germany, the King and Queen were blessed with a beautiful baby daughter. The little girl, whom they named Pirlipat, had golden hair and pretty white teeth.

Months before Princess Pirlipat was born, her parents had quarreled with the Mouse Queen. Because of their dispute, the Mouse Queen had sworn to cast an evil spell on Pirlipat. To keep this dreadful event from happening, the King and Queen had Pirlipat's cradle constantly guarded by six nursemaids, each one with a big cat on her lap.

One night all six nursemaids and all six cats fell asleep. The Mouse Queen, who had been waiting for just such a moment, turned the baby Princess into a horrible dwarf. In an instant, poor little Pirlipat's head became too large for her body, her mouth stretched from one ear to the other, and her chin wore a little white beard.

The court inventor and clockmaker, Drosselmeyer of Nuremberg, found that, to break the magic spell, the Princess must eat the kernel of the Krakatuk nut. He also found that the nut, which was so hard that even a cannon would not smash it, must be cracked in front of the Princess by a young man who had never worn boots and had never shaved. The young man must first crack the nut and then present it to the Princess with his eyes closed. Then he must take seven steps backwards without a misstep, keeping his eyes closed all the while.

Now that he knew how to break the spell, inventor Drosselmeyer set out to search for the Krakatuk nut. After searching for fifteen years, he gave up in despair and returned to Nuremberg. There, by a strange co-incidence, Drosselmeyer's brother found that he possessed one of the Krakatuks.

As the two brothers rejoiced at their discovery, they suddenly realized that Nathaniel Drosselmeyer, the inventor's nephew, was the right young man to crack the Krakatuk. Nathaniel had never shaved nor worn boots, and his favorite pastime was cracking nuts for the ladies. Surely, the brothers thought, Nathaniel would be able to break the spell and restore the Princess.

Nathaniel was immediately brought before Princess Pirlipat, where he easily broke the nutshell with his teeth. As the Princess ate the kernel, she became radiantly beautiful once more. But Nathaniel, who was taking the seven backward steps, tripped when the evil Mouse Queen ran between his feet. As he stumbled, she transformed him into an ugly wooden Nutcracker.

Nathaniel's uncle, who was horrified by this turn of events, asked the court astrologer what could be done to release Nathaniel from his Nutcracker enchantment. After the astrologer read the stars, he predicted that poor Nathaniel could be freed on two conditions. First, he must kill the seven-headed Mouse King, who was the son of the old Mouse Queen. Secondly, he must win the love of a lady who would care for him in spite of his ugliness. If these conditions were met, Nathaniel would regain his human form and rule as Prince of the Kingdom of Sweets.

The Nutcracker *auditions at the School of American Ballet.*

George Balanchine rehearsing children for his production of The Nutcracker.

When Christopher d'Amboise played the Nutcracker Prince, his father, dancer Jacques d'Amboise, coached him in the role.

THE NUTCRACKER CHILDREN

Every Christmas, a fairy tale comes to life for thousands of young dancers: They perform in *The Nutcracker* ballet. The children dance in hundreds of productions throughout the world.

The Nutcracker production that you see in this book is done by the New York City Ballet. When that company presents *The Nutcracker*, about forty children dance in each performance. The children take many different parts in the ballet, including the roles of Mary and Nathaniel, the young party guests, tin soldiers, angels, candy canes, and Polichinelles. Members of the New York City Ballet company take the other parts.

The young dancers who appear in this *Nutcracker* production study at the School of American Ballet in New York City. Each year the School holds special auditions for *The Nutcracker*, and most of the students try out. After several tense hours, about eighty children are chosen. When the children are given their parts, they are also assigned to an A cast or B cast. The two casts alternate for different performances.

With the auditions over, the work begins. In just a few weeks, the children must learn their parts, rehearse, have their costumes fitted, get new ballet slippers (the company pays for their shoes), and of course, maintain their regular school schedule.

Many young *Nutcracker* performers go on to professional dance careers, and some have even become the stars of today's ballet world. Suzanne Farrell, who began as an angel in *The Nutcracker*, now dances the Sugar Plum Fairy and other leading roles with the New York City Ballet.

George Balanchine, who founded the New York City Ballet and staged *The Nutcracker* for that company, appeared in the ballet many times as a young student in Russia. In different years, he played the parts of a candy cane, the Mouse King, and the Prince.

Margot Fonteyn, perhaps the greatest ballerina of this century, made her stage debut as a snowflake in *The Nutcracker* in 1934. As a student dancer with the Sadler's Wells Ballet Company in England, she was told to dance the "third snowflake of the second group on the left."

She was chosen for the part at the last minute, learned it in only two days, and went on stage feeling completely unprepared. In fact, she wasn't even sure where the audience was located. Luckily, the other snowflakes whispered directions ("forward," "turn," "follow me," and so on), and she muddled through the performance. As she recalls:

> It was something of a nightmare until we reached the point near the end where we all knelt in a group, waving our snowflake wands while paper snow rained about our heads. At this moment the opera chorus was singing, Tchaikovsky's inspired music had reached its most beguiling climax, the lights were dimmed to a soft blue, and the curtains swung gently together, muffling the applause on the other side. I felt an incredible elation; this was theatre, this was the real thing. . . . From this moment on, there could be no turning back.

At that performance, Margot Fonteyn found the inspiration that led her to a professional career. For her and for many other young dancers, *The Nutcracker* has truly cast a magic spell.